HOW THE SEA CAME TO BE

AND ALL THE CREATURES IN IT

WRITTEN BY JENNIFER BERNE

ILLUSTRATED BY AMANDA HALL

EERDMANS BOOKS FOR YOUNG READERS
GRAND RAPIDS, MICHIGAN

PART ONE

THE BIRTH OF THE SEA

Billions and billions of years long ago,
when the Earth was young and new,
the world was so hot, rock melted and boiled,
and fiery, wild winds blew.

Volcanoes exploded from inside the Earth.
They blazed and they blasted and boomed.
And comets and asteroids crashed out of the sky,
icy and rocky they zoomed.

Earth sizzled and simmered for millions of years.
It bubbled and burbled and hissed.
It raged and it rumbled, it thundered and boiled,
spewing lava and steamy hot mist.

Then slowly, so slowly, Earth started to cool.
And cooler and firmer it grew.
It heaved and it puckered. It wrinkled and bulged.
And crumpled and puckered anew.

The mountains grew tall, and the valleys dipped deep.
And steamy, hot clouds rose up high.
Dark clouds full of water encircled the world,
casting shadows to Earth from the sky.

And out of those clouds for the very first time,
rain started to fall to the ground.
For days and for nights, for thousands of years,
it thundered and rained and poured down.

It rained down the mountains, it rained down the rocks,
washing salt to the water below.
It rained oceans and oceans all over the world—
the first oceans so long, long ago.

And that was the birth of the sea.

PART TWO

THE BIRTH OF LIFE

The oceans flowed wide and the oceans flowed deep,
and bluer and clearer they grew.
And sunlight shone down on the face of the Earth,
this planet of watery blue.

Then something amazing, unseen, and so new
appeared in this shining blue sea . . .
The teeniest, tiniest stirrings of life
came to be, in the sea, came to be.

Though smaller than small, and adrift in the seas,
one became two became four.
For millions of years these first bits of life
became more, and then more, and then more.

A little twist here and a little turn there—
they combined and they grew and they changed.
And bigger and wider and longer they got
in new forms as they all rearranged.

There were ribbed and frilled creatures that wiggled and crawled,
catching a snack when they could.
And soft, spongy clusters that clung to the rocks,
sucking water to eat where they stood.

There were round jellyfish that drifted and squished
as they moved with a watery sigh,
trailing tentacle threads that would stick and would sting
and would capture the food floating by.

So to the sea came a new shape of life.
The form that it took was a worm,
with a head in the front and a tail on the back
and between—in the middle—a squirm.

For the very first time in this new world of ours,
was a creature that points as it squirms
with an idea of where it wanted to go—
to find food and to meet other worms.

Then there came creatures with hard armored shells
that crept on the very first feet.
And creatures with claws and antennae and teeth
to fight for the foods that they eat.

So to the ocean came all kinds of life—
fantastic, surprising, and new.
Step by step, bit by bit, they evolved in the sea.
And life grew, and life changed, and life grew.

And that was how life began in the sea.

PART THREE

ALL THAT THE SEA CAME TO BE . . .

FROM THEN TO NOW

Life grew and life spread in this salty sea world
for hundreds of millions of years.
From its surface above to its depths far below
where it's cold and all light disappears.

In the deep midnight zone, there live fish in the dark
with huge jaws and long, sharp, pointy teeth.
There they sit in the black, as they wait for the food
that drifts down to their world far beneath.

Just above, in the dim, almost dark, twilight zone,
there are fish oh-so-strange and yet real
who flash lights with their mouths or their heads or their tails
to trap creatures in search of a meal.

But where most sea life lives is the bright sunlit zone,
where the sun shines its rays and adds heat,
in the shallow blue seas, in the oceans so wide,
where light shimmers down hundreds of feet.

Every ocean is flowing with all kinds of life,
every shape, every size, every scale—
from the small shrimp-like plankton, too tiny to see,
to the mighty, gigantic blue whale.

There are fish that look silvery when seen from below
to disguise them as light from the sky.
Yet when seen from above, their dark speckles and spots
help them blend with the sea plants nearby.

Big flat flounders lie down with one side to the ground
and two eyes on the other—on top.
While the large schools of cod, trying not to get caught,
dip and swoop as they flip and they flop.

Watch the squid darting backwards with watery jets
as it hides in an inky black cloud.
And beware toothy sharks, barracudas, and eels,
a ferocious and dangerous crowd.

See the catfish and cowfish and lampreys and clams,
puffy blowfish and bluefish and snails.
Spiny lobsters and starfish and scallops and shrimp,
speedy sailfish and huge spouting whales.